World in Focus
France

HODDER
Wayland

CELIA TIDMARSH

First published in 2006 by Hodder Wayland,
an imprint of Hodder Children's Books

Commissioning editor: Victoria Brooker
Editor: Patience Coster
Inside design: Chris Halls, www.mindseyedesign.co.uk
Cover design: Hodder Wayland

Series concept and project management by EASI-Educational Resourcing
(info@easi-er.co.uk)
Statistical research: Anna Bowden

Maps and graphs: Martin Darlison, Encompass Graphics

British Library Cataloguing in Publication Data
Tidmarsh, Celia
France. - (World in focus)
1. France - Juvenile literature
I. Title
944'. 084

ISBN: 0750246901

Printed and bound in China

Hodder Children's Books
A division of Hodder Headline Limited
338 Euston Road, London NW1 3BH

Cover top: A bustling pavement café.
Cover bottom: The walled city of Carcassonne, southern France.
Title page: The traditional game of *pétanque*, or *boules*, is popular in France.

Picture acknowledgements. The author and publisher would like to thank the
following for allowing their pictures to be reproduced in this publication:
Corbis 10 (Free Agents Limited), 11 (Stefano Bianchetti), 17 (Owen Franken), 20 (Maurice
Rougemont/Corbis Sygma), 23 (Owen Franken), 24 (Jean Pierre Amet/Corbis Sygma), 31 (Frederic
Pitchal/Corbis Sygma), 32 (Owen Franken), 35 (Abdelfatah Belaid/Corbis Sygma), 36 (Reuters), 44 (Pierre
Schwartz), 48 (Gillian Darley;Edifice), 59 (Bernard Bisson/Corbis Sygma); Chris Fairclough Picture Library
cover top and *bottom*, 4, 5, 6, 8, 9, 12, 13, 14, 15, 16, 18, 19, 21, 22, 25, 26, 27, 28, 29, 30, 33, 34, 37, 38, 39, 40, 41,
42, 43, 45, 46, 47, 49, 50 and *title page*, 51, 52, 53, 54, 55, 56, 57 and 58.

The website addresses (URLs) included in this book were valid at the time of going to press.
However, because of the nature of the Internet, it is possible that some addresses may have
changed, or sites may have changed or closed down since publication. While the author and
Publishers regret any inconvenience this may cause the readers, no responsibility for any such
changes can be accepted by either the author or the Publisher.

The directional arrow portrayed on the map on page 7 provides only an approximation of north.
The data used to produce the graphics and data panels in this title were the latest available at the
time of production.

CONTENTS

CHAPTER 1

France –
An Overview

France is situated on the western edge of the European landmass. It is bordered by eight countries and has an extensive and varied coastline. France also governs eight overseas departments and territories located in the Caribbean and Indian and Pacific oceans.

THE PHYSICAL ENVIRONMENT

The physical landscape of France provides habitats for a wide variety of plants and animals. In general, France can be divided into two main regions. Towards the south and east are elevated plateaux and high mountains, including the Alps and the Pyrenees. Much of the north, west and centre of the country consists of broad plains and lowland hills and plateaux. Approximately 82 per cent of the land area is made up of farmland or forests, which provide an important natural resource to the French economy. Until around 1945, a large proportion of the French labour force (slightly less than a third) still worked on the land.

ECONOMICS AND POPULATION

In 2003, France was ranked as the world's fifth largest economy and one of its wealthiest countries, with a strong industrial and technological economy. During the second half of the twentieth century, agricultural employment declined rapidly. Today the majority of the workforce are employed in service industries and the professional and managerial sectors. France has a reputation for technological expertise and flair in areas such as the automobile and aircraft industries. Politically France plays a key role in international politics, mainly through its membership of organizations such as the European Union (EU), the North Atlantic Treaty Organization (NATO) and the United Nations (UN).

Did you know?

The French national anthem, 'La Marseillaise', gained its name because soldiers from the southern city of Marseille sang it in the streets of Paris during the French Revolution.

◀ The Côte d'Azur, named after the azure blue of the Mediterranean Sea, is a fine example of spectacular rocky coastline with headlands, bays and caves. The clifftops are covered by sparse vegetation, known as *maquis*.

▲ The Eiffel Tower, built in 1889, is perhaps one of the most famous of French landmarks. It is located in the centre of Paris and was named after its designer, Gustave Eiffel.

In 2004 the French population was around 60.4 million. This represents an increase of some 18.6 million people since 1950. The present day population is of mixed origins, reflecting the long history of settlement in France by different groups. Among the most influential of these groups were the Gauls (a fearsome Celtic people), and the Franks (a group of Germanic tribes), who gave France its name. Since the mid-twentieth century, France has witnessed immigration from its former colonial territories (particularly those in Africa) and, more recently, from Eastern Europe and Asia. The majority of French people (76 per cent in 2005) live in urban areas, with Paris, the capital, dominating in both size and influence. Like its people, France's settlements reflect their long history and represent a rich mix of architecture from Roman times through to the present day.

 Did you know?

The country of France is roughly the shape of a hexagon, and is sometimes referred to by its inhabitants as 'l'Hexagone'.

HISTORY AND CULTURE

French history is characterized by numerous changes in territory and leadership, many as the result of lengthy and bloody wars. Under the leadership of King Louis XVI (ruled 1774–92) and of Emperor Napoléon I (ruled 1799–1815), for example, France's borders extended to include areas that are today part of neighbouring Spain, Germany and Italy. France has also seen invasion from foreign powers, most notably during the two world wars of the twentieth century (1914–18 and 1939–45), during which some of the heaviest fighting took place on French soil. Between 1789 and 1794, France experienced a Revolution which transformed the system of government. This bloody conflict helped to establish the principle of the constitutional republic by which France is now governed.

France's rich cultural heritage has today spread far beyond its own borders. French food, fashion, art, cinema and architecture, for example, have become world renowned for quality and innovation. The French language, which was the language of international diplomacy in the seventeenth and eighteenth centuries, also has an influence beyond national boundaries and is spoken by many peoples around the world.

At the start of the twenty-first century, France's strong cultural and political position at the centre of Europe is under pressure from other European nations and broader global forces. How France adapts to these global and regional changes will play a major role in determining its future.

▼ Paris is a lively cosmopolitan city, with a thriving street culture. The many public open spaces attract pavement artists, musicians and jugglers.

Physical geography

- Land area: 545,630 sq km/210,668 sq miles
- Water area: 1,400 sq km/541 sq miles
- Total area: 547,030 sq km/211,208 sq miles
- World rank (by area): 49
- Land boundaries: 2,889 km/1,794 miles
- Border countries: Andorra, Belgium, Germany, Italy, Luxembourg, Monaco, Spain, Switzerland
- Coastline: 3,427 km/2,128 miles
- Highest point: Mt Blanc (4,807m/15,771 ft)

Lowest point: Rhone River Delta (-2 m/-7 ft)

Source: CIA World Factbook

 Did you know?

Denim originates from the town of Nîmes in southern France (denim is a contraction of '*de Nîmes*', meaning 'of Nîmes'). The blue fabric was first manufactured in Nîmes in the eighteenth century and was exported to California during the 1840s by a man called Levi Strauss, who used it to make hardwearing trousers for gold miners.

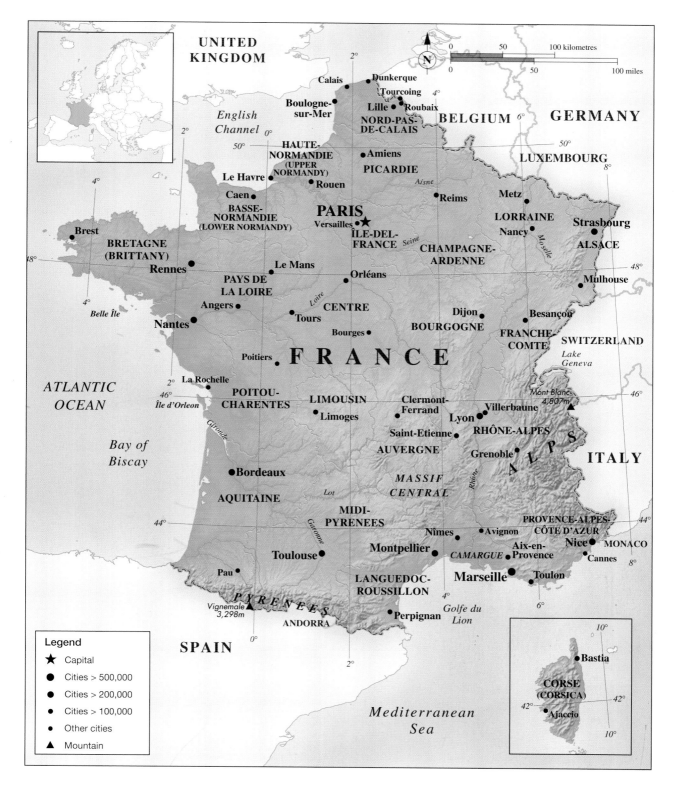

UNITED KINGDOM

BELGIUM

GERMANY

LUXEMBOURG

SWITZERLAND

ITALY

SPAIN

ANDORRA

MONACO

English Channel

ATLANTIC OCEAN

Bay of Biscay

Mediterranean Sea

Golfe du Lion

FRANCE

★ PARIS
Versailles
ÎLE-DEL-FRANCE

Calais
Dunkerque
Tourcoing
Boulogne-sur-Mer
Lille
Roubaix
NORD-PAS-DE-CALAIS

HAUTE-NORMANDIE (UPPER NORMANDY)
Le Havre
Caen
BASSE-NORMANDIE (LOWER NORMANDY)
Rouen
Amiens
PICARDIE
Aisne

Reims
Metz
LORRAINE
Nancy
Strasbourg
ALSACE
Moselle

Brest
BRETAGNE (BRITTANY)
Rennes
Belle Île

Le Mans
PAYS DE LA LOIRE
Angers
Nantes
Orléans
CENTRE
Tours
Bourges
Loire

Poitiers
POITOU-CHARENTES
La Rochelle
Île d'Orleon

CHAMPAGNE-ARDENNE
Seine

Dijon
BOURGOGNE
Besançon
FRANCHE-COMTE
Lake Geneva

LIMOUSIN
Limoges

Clermont-Ferrand
AUVERGNE
Saint-Etienne
Lyon
Villerbaune
RHÔNE-ALPES
Grenoble

Mont Blanc 4,807m ▲
A L P S
Rhône

Bordeaux
AQUITAINE
Gironde
Lot

MASSIF CENTRAL

MIDI-PYRENEES
Garonne
Toulouse
Pau

Vignemale ▲ 3,298m
P Y R E N E E S

Nîmes
Avignon
Montpellier
CAMARGUE
Aix-en-Provence
Marseille
Toulon
PROVENCE-ALPES-CÔTE D'AZUR
Nice
Cannes

LANGUEDOC-ROUSSILLON
Perpignan

CORSE (CORSICA)
Bastia
Ajaccio

0 50 100 kilometres
0 50 100 miles

Legend

★ Capital
● Cities > 500,000
● Cities > 200,000
• Cities > 100,000
• Other cities
▲ Mountain

CHAPTER 2

History

Prehistoric paintings in caves in the Périgord region of south-west France suggest that human settlement in France dates from around 15,000 BC. However, a more permanent record of human settlement can be traced back to the period of the Gauls, a Celtic people from central Europe who invaded the area from about 1,500 BC. They settled in a region that became known as Gaul, and developed trading links with the Greeks who had colonies on the Mediterranean coast.

In 52 BC, the Gauls were defeated by troops of the Roman emperor, Julius Caesar. The Roman Empire controlled Gaul until the fifth century AD, when it came under attack by tribes from northern Europe. One of these tribes, the Franks, eventually took control of the area and named it 'la Francie'.

The Frankish king, Charlemagne, ruled from AD 771 to 814 and expanded the French Empire into parts of Spain, Germany and northern Italy. Following Charlemagne's death, the French Empire was divided among his heirs. In AD 911, the Normans (Vikings from Scandinavia) took control of the area now known as Normandy in northern France. Other areas, such as Anjou, were taken over by the English. By AD 987, the Franks still ruled the kingdom of France but by then this was just a small area, comprising the present Île de France region.

CLAIMS TO THE THRONE

When William, duke of Normandy, invaded England in 1066 he seized areas of France that were under English rule. In 1154, William was succeeded to the English throne by Henry II, whose marriage to Eleanor of Aquitaine, the former queen of France, gave him control of large areas of south-west France. There followed long periods of conflict between the

◀ The exceptionally well preserved Roman aqueduct known as the Pont du Gard, near Avignon in the south of France, was once part of a 50-km (31-mile) long system of canals constructed around 19 BC to bring water from near Uzès to Nîmes. The Pont du Gard has 35 arches in the upper tier.

English and the French. In 1328, Charles IV of France died with no obvious heir. His nephew, the English king Edward III, was enraged when the French throne was given to Charles' grandson, Philippe de Valois.

Edward's claim to the French throne led to the Hundred Years' War (1337–1453). For much of the War the English had the upper hand, defeating the French at the Battle of Agincourt in 1415 and taking control of Paris in 1420. However, in 1429 a young peasant girl named Joan of Arc claimed that God had told her to urge on the French troops to victory. She is credited with turning the war in France's favour by inspiring French soldiers with her

divine message. In 1429, Charles VII was crowned king of France; in 1436, the French recaptured Paris; and, by 1453, the English had been driven from most French territory.

INFLUENCES OF RENAISSANCE AND RELIGION

Between 1494 and 1559, France waged wars with Italy over territory. At this time, a movement known as the Renaissance was taking place in Italy. During the reign of Francis I (1515–47) many Italian ideas about culture were brought to France. Francis I invited the Italian artist Leonardo da Vinci to France, and the artist brought his painting of the Mona Lisa, which still hangs in the Louvre museum in Paris today.

Did you know?

In Brittany, standing stones and burial mounds dating from between 5,700 BC and 1,000 BC have been found around the town of Carnac.

▼ The Cathedral of Notre Dame in Paris took more than 180 years to build and was completed in 1345. It was one of the first cathedrals built in the Gothic style with many elaborate features, including flying buttresses and stained glass windows.

Between 1562 and 1598, the Wars of Religion took place within France between Huguenots (French Protestants) and Catholics. In 1598, King Henri IV ended the wars by passing a law known as the Edict of Nantes, granting religious freedom to all French subjects.

FROM THE BOURBONS TO REVOLUTION

Between 1598 and 1792, France was ruled by the Bourbon dynasty. One of its greatest leaders was King Louis XIV (ruled 1643–1715), who led France to become the dominant power in Europe. Louis waged military campaigns to gain new French territories, such as Canada and the Louisiana territory in North America. There was a period of industrialization and innovation in France. Louis XIV used France's wealth to build a vast chateau at Versailles, to which he relocated the royal court from Paris. Towards the end of his reign, Louis involved France in the disastrous War of the Spanish Succession (1701–14). This was an attempt to establish a Bourbon king on the Spanish throne. Other European countries, including England and Italy, opposed this extension of French power. In 1714, the Treaty of Utrecht ended the war by allowing the Bourbon King Philip V to take the Spanish throne but only if he broke his connection with the French throne.

France suffered further military defeats under Louis XV (ruled 1715–74). These included the loss of French colonies in Canada, the West Indies and India to the British. Louis XVI (ruled 1774–92) tried to avenge the loss of these territories by siding with the colonists against Britain in the American War of Independence (1778–83). The French people were heavily taxed to pay for this expensive military venture, and this resulted in widespread poverty in France. The situation contributed to a growing resentment of the ruling élite.

◀ The French king, Louis XIV, moved his court to the Chateau de Versailles in 1682. Versailles is about 20 km (12 miles) from the centre of Paris.

▲ In this nineteenth-century painting, royalist troops battle to defend the Bastille prison in Paris from angry crowds on 14 July, 1789.

By 1789, public unrest had erupted into a popular revolution. The people formed a National Assembly which refused to disband until a constitution was drawn up giving rights to ordinary French citizens. On 14 July, the king's troops attempted to disperse the Assembly, but the action backfired. Crowds stormed the Bastille prison in Paris, a symbol of the oppressive rule of the king. A period of great bloodshed followed and many 'enemies of the Revolution', including nobles and the king and queen, were beheaded. By 1792, France had a new constitution and was declared a republic. However, social unrest continued until 1794, during which time many of those suspected of opposing the Revolution were assassinated. A new form of parliamentary government emerged from this period, but there was a lingering public distrust of the new political leaders. Against this background, Napoléon Bonaparte came to power in 1799.

 Did you know?

The guillotine was a machine designed to behead privileged nobles, including members of the royal family, during the French Revolution of 1789. Large crowds would gather to watch the public executions.

▲ Napoléon Bonaparte commissioned the Arc de Triomphe in1806 to commemorate his military victories. But Napoléon began to lose battles and by 1813 he was no longer the emperor of France. The Arc was completed in the 1830s. It is one of the main landmarks in Paris, located at the meeting point of twelve broad avenues.

NAPOLÉON BONAPARTE

Napoléon Bonaparte was a general in the French army during the Revolution. In 1799 he took control of the government in a military coup and, in the following years, consolidated his power through military actions against Austria and Britain. In 1804 Napoléon declared himself Emperor of France, and by 1812 his armies controlled most of western and central mainland Europe. However, Napoléon's invasion of Russia in 1812 ended in defeat. Several nations formed an alliance against France, and Napoléon was defeated at the

Battle of the Nations at Leipzig, Germany, in 1813. He was forced into exile.

In 1815 Napoléon returned to France and ruled for a further 'Hundred Days' before he was again defeated, this time by the British, at the Battle of Waterloo. He was exiled to the remote island of St Helena, where he died in 1824. Still remembered by many French people as a national hero, Napoléon made important changes to the government of France. For example, he ensured that the legal system incorporated principles from the French Revolution, such as the recognition of an individual's right to own property.

WORLD WAR

In the early twentieth century, France was invaded during the First World War (1914–18). More than one million young French soldiers were killed in the trenches, and large areas of north-west France, including farmland and villages, were devastated. In the Second World War (1939–45) France was occupied by Germany in 1940; it was liberated in 1944 by the combined forces of the Allies and the Free French.

The Fourth Republic (1946–58) was founded following the Second World War and lasted until 1958, when a war of independence in the French colony of Algeria caused a crisis. The war had begun in 1954; by 1956 more than 400,000 French troops were fighting in Algeria and there was no sign of an end to the conflict. As members of the government, under President René Coty, argued among themselves about what to do, other politicians and army officers staged a coup. Coty was replaced by former president, General Charles de Gaulle, who established the Fifth Republic in 1958 and brought the war to an end in 1962.

PEACE AND PROSPERITY

After the Second World War, the French government adopted economic and political policies to restore prosperity and peace. One of the most ambitious of these was the joint creation with Germany of the European Coal and Steel Community in 1951. This early trading agreement later evolved and expanded to become the European Economic Community (EEC) in 1957, an organization that was renamed the European Union (EU) in 1993. In 2005, the EU had a membership of 25 countries.

The prosperity enjoyed by France over the last half century can, in part at least, be attributed to the success of these institutions. Whether the

expanded EU will continue to serve France's future so well remains to be seen. Certainly the French people seemed to have lost faith in the EU when they voted against the proposed EU constitution in May 2005. This led to the resignation of the prime minister, Jean Pierre Raffarin, and to much debate between and within the other member countries of the EU.

Focus on: The French Republics

Transition from one republic to the next has been brought about by political upheavals such as a period of absolute rule (for example, between the First and Second Republics) or a coup to remove an unpopular leader (for example between the Fourth and Fifth). Each republic is marked by some changes to the constitution, although the fundamental principles of the French Revolution have been left in place throughout. The five republics are:

First Republic 1792–1804
Second Republic 1848–1852
Third Republic 1870–1940
Fourth Republic 1946–1958
Fifth Republic 1958–present

▶ In northern France there are hundreds of cemeteries filled with the graves of people who died in the First World War.

CHAPTER 3

Landscape and Climate

France is Europe's third largest country (after Russia and the Ukraine), covering an area of 547,030 sq km (211,208 sq miles). It is approximately twice the size of the UK, or the US state of Colorado. It shares land borders with eight countries and is bounded by the Atlantic Ocean to the west, the Mediterranean Sea to the south and the English Channel (*La Manche*) to the north.

MASSIFS AND MOUNTAINS

The physical landscape ranges from low, rolling plains to high, rugged mountains. While about 60 per cent of France is below 250 m (820 feet) in altitude, the remaining 40 per cent is a spectacular highland landscape.

The oldest of the highlands are the 'massifs', formed between 345 and 225 million years ago. The Massif Central covers some 91,000 sq km (35,135 sq miles) of south-central France and is famous for its chain of extinct volcanoes, including the Puy de Dôme which is 1,465 m (4,806 feet) high. Other mountainous regions in France include the Alps, the Jura and the Pyrenees. Formed 50 million years ago, these are geologically younger mountains than the massifs and are generally more rugged and higher. The French Alps include Mont Blanc which, at 4,807 m (15,771 feet), is the highest peak in Europe. The Pyrenees reach a maximum height of 3,404 m (11,168 ft) and the Jura reach 1,723 m (5,653 feet).

◀ The landscape of France is fantastically varied and includes high plateaux (left), rugged mountains and vast, rolling plains.

▲ The Loire River rises in the Cévennes and drains into the Bay of Biscay. Along its course it flows through pretty towns like Amboise, above.

RIVERS AND COASTS

France is drained by five large river systems. The Loire is the longest river, stretching 1,012 km (629 miles) from the Massif Central to the Atlantic coast. The Garonne also flows into the Atlantic, with tributaries draining much of south-west France, including the Pyrenees. The Rhône links Lake Geneva in the Alps with the Mediterranean Sea, and is joined at Lyon by the River Saône. The remaining two major systems are the Rhine, forming part of the border between France and Germany, and the Seine which passes through Paris before draining into the English Channel.

France has an immensely varied coastline some 3,427 km (2,128 miles) long. There are salt marshes around the estuary of the Rhône on the Mediterranean coast, sand dunes on the Atlantic coast south of Bordeaux, chalk cliffs on the Normandy coast and rocky beaches in Brittany and on the Côte d'Azur. The fan-shaped mouth of the River Rhône, where it flows into the Mediterranean, is a fine example of a delta.

? Did you know?

The official height of Mont Blanc varies because of the changing thickness of the ice and snow on its highest peak. It was measured at 4,807 m (15,771 feet) in 1894, 4,810 m (15,782 feet) in 2001 and again at 4,807 m (15,771 feet) in 2004.

VARIATIONS IN THE CLIMATE

Generally France has a temperate climate with mild winters, although climatic variations do exist within the country as a result of the proximity of the sea. Western France is usually wetter because the prevailing winds bring moisture from the Atlantic Ocean. Also, during the winter months, warm ocean currents pass close to the west coast so temperatures are higher than those of inland regions. Eastern France can be very cold in winter and very hot in the summer. This is because the vast European landmass heats up and cools down more quickly than the sea. Altitude is also an influence on climate in France. Mountainous areas are generally cooler because the temperature falls by around 1°C (1.8°F) for every 150 m (492 feet) of altitude. This is known as the lapse rate. Northern France is situated between latitudes 42°N and 52°N, which makes it generally cooler than the south.

EXTREME WEATHER AND CLIMATIC EVENTS

Extreme weather and climatic events do not occur very frequently but can cause problems on occasions. In 2003, for example, much of France experienced a record-breaking summer with a heatwave and the worst drought for 25 years. This was followed in the south-east of the country by serious winter flooding caused by torrential rainfall. Some climatologists believe that such extreme climatic events are becoming more frequent because of global warming.

The events of 2003 would normally be considered rare by climatologists and it was unusual that they occurred in the same year. There are possible explanations other than

▼ Dairy cattle graze in the lush, green pastures of Normandy, northern France, where the climate is generally wetter than the south.

global warming, however. In the south-east of France, for instance, the clearance of natural vegetation to build more houses and roads is thought to have reduced the ability of the ground to absorb water during periods of heavy rainfall. Instead the rain flows rapidly into rivers that may be unable to cope and are thus more likely to flood.

▲ Variations in the French climate mean that vines grow in the sunny and generally frost-free south.

Focus on: The Mistral

The Mistral is a wind that blows down the Rhône Valley for about 100 days every year, usually in winter and early spring. It is an example of a katabatic wind, caused when cold, dense air from mountainous areas flows downhill and replaces the relatively warmer, lighter air in the lower-lying valleys. In the case of the Mistral, cold air from the Massif Central spills into the Rhône Valley and is channelled southwards to the Mediterranean. The Mistral is a cold, dry and gusty wind; it occasionally reaches force 10 and can damage buildings and uproot trees. It is thought by some local people to affect people's moods. Those people who live in its path often report of depression, headaches and irritability.

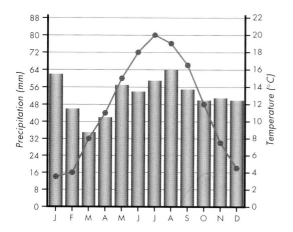

▲ Average monthly climate conditions in Paris

CHAPTER 4

Population and Settlements

In 2004, the French population was about 60.4 million, with a further 1.7 million in overseas territories. Between 1950 and 1980, the population surged from 41.8 million to 53.8 million. In common with other western European countries, this growth has slowed as the fertility rate (the average number of children born to each woman) has fallen. In 1964 it was just under 3 and by 2001 it had fallen to 1.9. This trend, combined with higher life expectancy, has led to a gradual ageing of the population with an increasing proportion of people aged over 65 years.

AN AGEING POPULATION

Today, 16 per cent of the French population is over 65, and this figure is expected to rise to 33 per cent by 2040. The government is concerned about the demands that an ageing population may place on health and social services. The ratio of the working age population (which generates taxes to pay for health and social services) to the older, retired population is declining. This situation could be improved by people working beyond the official retirement age of 60, or by a future change in the retirement age to extend people's working lives. Also, modern technology and industry are more productive than they once were. This means that, although there may be fewer workers, they will generate the same, and often higher, incomes to support an ageing population.

▼ In general, French people over 65 are fitter and in better health than used to be the case. In retirement they may have more time to pursue leisure interests and to socialize.

A MIX OF PEOPLES

France's population comprises people from many different origins, reflecting a long history of immigration. During the twentieth century, France brought about two main phases of immigration to meet the need for labour. After the First World War many people were allowed to migrate from other European countries, such as Italy and Poland, to fill the gap that the war deaths had left in the workforce. There was a similar need following the Second World War, although this time migrants came mainly from Portugal and North African countries, like Tunisia and Algeria, which were once French colonies. Since 1974, France has experienced rising unemployment and has therefore placed stricter controls on immigration. Most of the migrants allowed entry to France since 1974 have been those with close family members already resident there.

When migrants take French citizenship they are considered to have shed their cultural differences. This means that no official records are kept of migrants' country of origin and there are no government statistics showing how many immigrants have settled in France. Despite this policy of assimilation, differences do exist. For example, immigrants from North Africa brought Islam to France and there are now at least six million Muslims in France. Music and food from North Africa are also enjoyed by the wider French society.

Cultural and religious differences are the focus for occasional tensions between ethnic minority groups and extreme right-wing members of French society. In 2002 these tensions became national news when Jean-Marie Le Pen, leader of the right-wing Le Front National (National Front) Party, gained some support in presidential elections for his stand on immigration into France, which he promised to end completely. He and his followers blamed immigration for high unemployment (although immigrants usually take on the low-paid unskilled jobs that other French citizens do not want). Ultimately there was not enough support for Le Pen to win him the presidency.

▲ The mix of ethnic origins is represented on the streets of Paris where many migrants from different cultures live and work.

 Did you know?

Ethnic minorities in France are more likely to suffer social problems than the majority population. Young North Africans, for example, have a 40 per cent unemployment rate compared to 10 per cent of young adults in the general population.

WHERE PEOPLE LIVE

On average, population density in France is 110 people per sq km (286 per sq mile). There are huge variations between regions, however, and highly urbanized areas, such as Paris, are far more densely populated than rural areas, such as the Auvergne. Around 40 per cent of France is sparsely populated and suffers from economic and social problems such as lack of jobs and services (for example, hospitals and post offices). The worst affected areas run in a band from the north-east to the south-west of France, known as the 'empty diagonal'. These areas are declining further as young people migrate to regions that offer more opportunities. The government is trying to tackle these problems by encouraging jobs and income generation. One example of this is the availability of government grants for people who want to convert disused farm buildings into second homes.

In France, any settlement with a population of more than 5,000 is classified as urban. By this definition, around 76 per cent of the population lives in urban areas. Today many of the largest cities are losing their populations to nearby villages and smaller towns. This is because many people want to escape the stresses of city life, such as air pollution and traffic congestion. Improved public transport means that many of those leaving the city still commute to city jobs, but others are finding new employment in their home settlements. Some villages have adopted strategies to encourage this trend. For example, Neuvy-le-Roi, near Tours, has turned part of its school into a centre for small-scale, local businesses and services, and has helped create 150 jobs in five years.

 Did you know?

The region of the Île de France, in which Paris is located, covers only 2 per cent of the country's area, but is home to 20 per cent of the French population.

▲ This photo of Annecy in central south-east France shows the traditional older style of housing typical of many French towns and cities.

Population data

- Population: 60.4 million
- Population 0-14 yrs: 19%
- Population 15-64 yrs: 65%
- Population 65+ yrs: 16%
- Population growth rate: 0.5%
- Population density: 110.4 per sq km/ 286.0 per sq mile
- Urban population: 76%
- Major cities: Lyon 1,408,000
    Marseille 1,384,000
    Paris 9,854,000

Source: United Nations and World Bank

◀ Although the majority of people live in towns and cities, there are still many villages in rural areas. This one in the south of France has old houses of traditional architecture that are clustered around the church.

Paris is France's largest city, with a population of around 2 million in the older central area and a further 7.8 million in the wider metropolitan area. The growth of Paris has caused problems, such as serious traffic congestion. Since the 1960s, various urban development schemes have encouraged the relocation of offices and services away from the central area to relieve congestion. The new national library, for example, is located in Tolbiac, a previously underdeveloped district of eastern Paris.

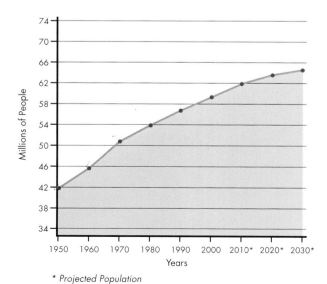

Projected Population

▲ Population growth 1950-2030

Focus on: Problems of urban deprivation

Between 1950 and 1970 many immigrants arriving to work in France were housed in estates that were built quickly and cheaply, often as high-rise blocks of flats, on the edges of cities such as Marseille and Lyon. These estates, such as the Petit Bard estate in Montpellier, are now very run-down because little or no maintenance work has been carried out since they were first built. Their populations are still overwhelmingly made up of the immigrants (mainly North Africans) who first settled there and they have some of the lowest incomes, highest unemployment rates and the lowest levels of literacy (as low as 66 per cent) in France.

CHAPTER 5

Government and Politics

France is a democratic republic, with an elected president and members of the National Assembly and Senate, which make up Parliament. The National Assembly is the main decision-making body, while the Senate's power is limited. The president is elected for a five-year term, as are the 577 deputies who make up the National Assembly.

As head of state, the president holds considerable power, particularly in relation to foreign policy. He or she chooses the prime minister, although the latter must be selected from deputies who represent the majority party in the National Assembly. As head of the government, the prime minister then chooses the government ministers.

The president and prime minister may represent different political parties. This occurred between 1997 and 2002, when President Jacques Chirac of the right-wing l'Union Pour un Movement Populaire (Union for a Popular Movement) worked alongside Prime Minister Lionel Jospin of the left-wing La Parti Socialiste (Socialist Party). This situation is known as 'cohabitation'.

LOCAL GOVERNMENT

The local government of France is divided into five tiers. There are 22 *régions* (regions) that are divided into 100 *départements*

▼ The Palais de Luxembourg, Paris, built in 1631, is now home to the French Senate.

 The National Assembly of Deputies meets in Paris. They take their seats in the semi-circular chamber to the left or right of the centre, according to their political allegiance.

(departments), further divided into 342 *arrondisements*. The last two, smallest, tiers are the 4,054 *cantons* and 36,763 *communes*. Traditionally, central government has appointed a *prefect* (leader) to head the various *départements*. However, in 1982, 1986 and 2003 changes were made to the law as part of a process of decentralization. Now much of the *prefect*'s power over transport, tourism, economic development and education has been transferred to locally elected departmental councils. These are also entitled to call referenda on particular local issues to give local people more of a say in their government.

POLITICAL PARTIES

There is a wide range of political parties in France, from far left to far right. For general elections, parties will often merge into coalitions to increase their support base. At the time of the 1997 election, for example, there was a coalition of the *gauche plurielle* (the broad left) formed by the Socialists, the Greens and other left-wing parties. Since 1958, when the present constitution was adopted, there have been both right- and left-wing presidents and governments. Until recently, popular support tended to favour the middle ground of politics rather than the extremes of left or right. However, in the presidential election of 2002, Jean-Marie Le Pen, leader of the far right party, Le Front National, was voted through to the second round of the election to face Jacques Chirac. In between the first and second round elections many French people took to the streets to demonstrate against Le Pen and his racist policies. In the second round, Chirac won by the largest margin (82 per cent to 19 per cent) ever recorded at this stage of a presidential election.

Did you know?

France has four *régions d'outre-mer* (overseas regions) which hold the same status as metropolitan French regions. They are Guadeloupe, French Guiana, Martinique and Réunion.

THE CONSTITUTION

The French constitution draws on principles from the *Declaration of the Rights of Man*, a document written in 1789 by radicals during the Revolution. The constitution establishes France as a secular and democratic republic. It also promotes a strong sense of French identity, stating that all citizens are equal, regardless of origin, race, religion, culture or language. Sometimes elements of the constitution can cause problems. For example, it is stated that the republic's language is French. This means there can be no official recognition of regional languages in areas like Brittany and Corsica. Since the start of the Fifth Republic in 1958, the constitution has been amended several times. In 1997, for example, the government approved equal representation for men and women in political posts. However, while the percentage of women deputies in the National Assembly has doubled since 1996, it is still low. In 2002, only 12 per cent of deputies were women.

Focus on: Referendum in Corsica

In 2003, Corsica held a referendum on whether to accept greater independence from central government. It was hoped that a 'yes' outcome would end more than 30 years of violent campaigns, including bombings and the murder of a government *prefect*, carried out by groups demanding independence from France. Although those carrying out the violence are a small minority, the people of Corsica have a strong sense of regional identity. For a long time the French government's view has been that granting autonomy or independence to Corsica would undermine the constitution and threaten the unity of France. However, in recognition of the general trend towards decentralization, President Chirac changed his mind and gave his support to the referendum proposal. The outcome of the vote was extremely close, with 50.98 per cent voting 'no'.

▼ A local politician campaigns for votes in Corsica. A considerable number of Corsicans oppose the dominance of French language and culture and want independence from central government.

FRANCE AND THE EU

As a founding member of the European Union, France has influenced and been influenced by various EU policies. French governments and the French people have generally been positive about the role the EU plays in political and economic life. In 2002, France adopted the common currency of the Euro. There have been issues of conflict, however. For example, in 1999 France signed the European Charter on Regional and Minority Languages. Following this, the Conseil Constitutionel, France's highest court, ruled that the charter undermined the French constitution, which states that the Republic's language is French.

The enlargement of the EU, from 15 to 25 countries in 2004, is challenging France's role within it. There are also further applications for membership from other countries. In particular, Turkey's application to join the EU is opposed by about two thirds of French voters, partly because of fears that Turkish immigrants will take jobs from French citizens.

French people seemed to be turning against the EU when, in May 2005, 55 per cent voted in a referendum to reject the proposed EU constitution. Some analysts believe this was more to do with voters wanting to show their disapproval of domestic policies, such as the reform of the health system, rather than an outright rejection of the principles of the EU. However, the French referendum result has raised many questions about the future of the EU, and France's position within it.

▼ In common with other economically developed countries, France has many immigrants who do unskilled, low-paid jobs that are essential to the economy. But some French voters fear that their jobs might be lost to immigrant workers.

CHAPTER 6

Energy and Resources

France is a highly industrialized country, and it accounts for approximately 2.5 per cent of the world's total energy consumption. Since 1980, the consumption rate has risen steadily, from 8.5 quadrillion BTU (quads) to 10.5 quads in 2001. Consumption per head of population, at 178 million BTU per capita, is high compared with neighbouring western European countries, such as the UK (142 million BTU). However, it is still much lower than the USA, which consumes 342 million BTU per capita.

THE PROBLEM OF DEPENDENCY

France has few natural energy resources. Until the 1970s, coal provided about 20 per cent of primary (total) fuel needs and 46 per cent of generated electricity. However, France's coal reserves are now either exhausted or too expensive to access at present and its last mines were closed in 2004. France's primary energy requirements are now met by oil, nuclear energy and natural gas.

Until the mid 1970s, oil provided 77 per cent and nuclear energy only 5 per cent of requirements. When oil producers increased their prices in 1973, the French government reduced oil imports and increased the use of nuclear energy. Uranium was mined in France, so the country had more control over this energy source. Domestic uranium deposits are now much depleted, but nuclear energy is still regarded as a relatively independent energy source. French companies mine deposits in Niger, Canada, Australia and Kazakhstan, so France still has some control over this vital resource. In 2004, France was using 2.04 million barrels of oil a day (bbl/d), of which 1.96 million bbl/d was imported from Saudi Arabia and Norway. About 97 per cent of the natural gas consumed in France is imported from Norway, Russia and Algeria.

▼ France imports crude oil and gas that are then refined for different uses within the country. This oil refinery is at Dunkerque on the northern coast.

Energy data

- Energy consumption as % of world total: 2.5%
- Energy consumption by sector (% of total):

Industry:	30
Transportation:	31
Agriculture:	2
Services:	13
Residential:	24

- CO_2 emissions as % of world total: 1.6
- CO_2 emissions per capita in tonnes p.a.: 6.1

Source: World Resources Institute

THE NUCLEAR ENERGY DILEMMA

France has the second largest nuclear power capacity in the world, after the USA. Nuclear energy provides 81 per cent of the country's electricity (in 1984 it provided 15 per cent). The electricity produced is relatively cheap and exceeds France's needs, so some is exported to neighbouring countries. France is now the largest electricity exporter in the European Union.

A benefit of nuclear energy, as opposed to fossil fuels, is that it does not release greenhouse gases (carbon, sulphur dioxide and nitrous oxides) when burned. However, the French public are increasingly worried about the safety of nuclear energy, particularly the disposal of radioactive waste. The government had planned for nuclear power to generate all electricity, but these plans are being reconsidered as public opposition to the nuclear option grows.

▲ This nuclear power station is in the Rhône-Alpes region of central south-eastern France.

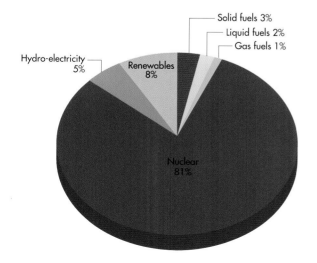

▲ Energy generation by source

Focus on: Renewable energy

With the exception of hydro-electric power (HEP), renewable energy sources have yet to be commercially developed in France. The government target is to provide 21 per cent from renewable sources by 2010. HEP currently provides 5 per cent of this, but its potential has already been fully developed in areas where the natural conditions are suitable, for example on the fast-flowing rivers of the Massif Central. A tidal barrage to generate electricity has been built across the Rance estuary in Normandy. In 2001, power from biomass, geothermal, solar and wind accounted for less than 1 per cent of the country's overall energy consumption. With further investment from the French government and commercial companies, there is scope for development in all these areas.

MINERAL RESOURCES

France used to be an important producer of iron ore, bauxite, uranium and coal. However, by 2004, mining of these minerals had ceased. Increased imports of cheaper raw materials, lower prices as a result of greater competition, and the depletion of mineral reserves all contributed to the closure of French mines. Another factor was the removal of subsidies by the French government (as a result of EU policies). Subsidies had artificially been keeping unprofitable mines open.

FORESTRY

Timber is an important natural resource and forests cover 9.3 million hectares (22.9 million acres), approximately 17 per cent of the land area. Two thirds of the forests are deciduous, including beech and oak. Pine is the most common coniferous type. The Office Nationale des Forêts (ONF) manages the forests owned nationally and by local authorities. About 70 per cent of forested area is owned and managed privately. The annual harvest from nationally owned forests is about 34 million cubic metres (1,201 million cubic feet) of timber.

Environmentalists criticize the ONF for giving the commercial use of timber a higher priority than conservation. Forests also provide beautiful natural environments that are enjoyed by tourists and generate tourist revenue.

▼ Logging operations like this one near Montauban provide jobs in rural areas where there may be few alternative types of employment.

▲ Small fishing boats, such as these at St Brieuc in Brittany, are owned and operated by individuals or families rather than companies.

FISHING

Fish consumption in France has risen steadily from about 15 kg (33 lbs) per capita in the 1970s to 26 kg (57 lbs) per capita in the late 1990s. France's fisheries produce about 750,000 tonnes (738,000 tons) per year, with a value of 0.14 per cent of the Gross Domestic Product (GDP). This relatively small contribution conceals the significance of fishing as an economic activity in coastal regions. There are more than 8,000 vessels in the fishing fleets that work around the coasts of France and its overseas *départements* and territories. French fleets fish off the eastern coast of Canada because two islands (Saint-Pierre and Miquelon) still remain French territory.

The operation and range of French fishing fleets are affected by European Union policies and international agreements. In 1983, the introduction of a Common Fisheries Policy meant that member states were required to conserve and manage fish stocks. France has also signed international agreements, including those creating Exclusive Economic Zones (EEZs). These are maritime areas of 370 km (200 nautical miles) from the coast in which the coastal state has rights over the living resources of the sea. Until the EEZs, it was assumed that the ocean's resources should be free for all to use. The EEZ over which France has rights is 11 million sq km (4.2 million sq miles), made up of 260,000 sq km (100,386 sq miles) around metropolitan France and over 10 million sq km (4 million sq miles) around overseas *départements* and territories.

 Did you know?

Bauxite, the raw material for aluminium, took its name from Les Baux, near the town of Arles in Provence in southern France. Bauxite was first discovered there in 1821.

CHAPTER 7

Economy and Income

France is the world's fifth largest economy with a Gross National Income (GNI) of US\$ 1,523 billion. This economic strength is built upon a highly skilled workforce, a range of manufacturing industries and substantial agricultural resources. In terms of employment, the services sector has become most significant, providing over 72 per cent of all jobs (as opposed to 58 per cent in 1980). Since 1980, employment in manufacturing has declined from 33 per cent to 25 per cent, and agriculture now provides only 3 per cent of jobs, compared with nearly 9 per cent in 1980. Imported minerals, such as uranium, are still processed in France and this provides some employment, although it is less than 1 per cent of the labour force.

SERVICES SECTOR

The expanding services sector includes banking, insurance, architecture, transport, and welfare services such as education and health. Tourism is a major service industry. France is one of the world's most popular tourist destinations with 75 million foreign visitors arriving in 2003, generating US\$ 64.5 billion. France has also successfully developed high technology and telecommunications industries. The French government finances about 48 per cent of the research carried out in these fields.

MANUFACTURING

Jobs have been lost in traditional manufacturing industries, such as shipbuilding, because of competition from abroad, for example, South Korea and China where labour costs are cheaper. Also domestic raw materials, for example iron ore, have

▼ In France's industrial heartlands, heavy goods are still transported by barge.

become exhausted and this has led to the closure of many of the industries dependent on them. However, some economically important industries still thrive. France is the world's third major car manufacturer, with two major companies, Peugeot-Citroën and Renault producing 5.5 million vehicles in 2001. Much of the steel used is produced in France and other French companies supply car parts, for example, tyres are supplied by Michelin, a company based in Clermont-Ferrand. The aeronautics industry, Matra-Aérospatiale, part of the European Airbus consortium, is also particularly successful. In 2003 it sold more than 300 planes, overtaking Boeing as the world's largest producer of civil aircraft.

AGRICULTURE

Agriculture has declined in terms of employment. In the past farming was very important with many people working the land. Over the past 40 years this has changed, largely as a result of the EU's Common Agricultural Policy (CAP). The CAP encouraged increased mechanization and use of fertilizers. This led to higher production and fewer people needed to work the land. France is the second largest food producer in the world, after the USA. Over 70 per cent of France's agricultural output is processed and its foodstuffs industry is the country's third largest employer.

? Did you know?

As a member of the EU, around 70 per cent of France's trade is with other EU countries.

Economic data

- Gross National Income (GNI) in US$: 1,523,024,527,360
- World rank by GNI: 5
- GNI per capita in US$: 24,770
- World rank by GNI per capita: 23
- Economic growth: 0.1%

Source: World Bank

▲ A worker at the car manufacturer Renault's assembly line in Romorantin in central France.

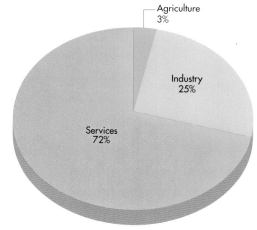

Agriculture 3%

Industry 25%

Services 72%

▲ Contribution by sector to national income

▲ A wine chemist at work. In France today, working women are generally better qualified academically than their male counterparts.

UNEMPLOYMENT

Although France has a strong economy, there are also some economic problems. Unemployment is higher than in many other European Union countries. In 2002, the unemployment rate was 8.8 per cent compared with 5.2 per cent in the UK and 2.9 per cent in the Netherlands. Since 1980, the rate for people under the age of 25 has risen from 15.5 per cent to 21 per cent.

The government has tried to tackle unemployment, for example, by introducing a 35-hour working week. The idea of this was to create more jobs by restricting the hours of those already in work. However, although more than 200,000 extra jobs were created between 1997 and 2000, some economics experts have argued that the hours restriction has actually worsened overall unemployment by making France less competitive in the global economy. In 2005, despite the fact that 69 per cent of the French public opposed the change, the government voted to extend the working week to 48 hours. Workers are not legally required to work 48 hours a week, but now companies can demand that they do.

 Did you know?

On 1 January 2002, France, along with most other member countries of the EU, dropped its national currency in favour of the Euro. Twelve of the 25 member countries have adopted the Euro, while many of the latest members, who joined in 2004, have applied for adoption.

REGIONAL INEQUALITIES

There are significant economic differences between geographical areas in France. The four largest urban areas – Paris, Lyon, Marseille and Lille – have 42 per cent of the country's population and a high share of the total economic activity. In contrast, many rural areas in the south and south-east are suffering from economic decline. Traditionally these rural areas were dependent on farming but, in France as a whole, the number of farms has declined from 1,017,000 in 1988 to about 664,000 in 2000. When older farmers retire there is no one to take over because younger people are moving to more prosperous areas in search of work. The economic problems of poor rural areas are being tackled in a number of ways. Subsidies have been introduced so that smaller farms can continue, and rural business centres have been created to advise and assist farmers.

▲ This traditional farmhouse near Aurillac in south-central France is surrounded by sunflowers that are grown for their oil.

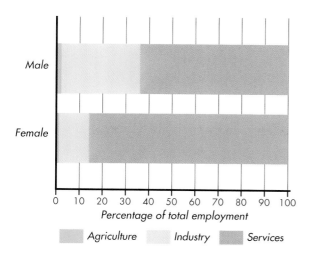

▲ Labour force by sector and gender

Percentage of total employment

Agriculture   Industry   Services

Focus on: Women in the workforce

The number of women who go out to work has increased steadily. The main reason for this is that women are now more likely to continue with employment after they marry and become mothers. Improvements to education mean that, by 1998, 44 per cent of full-time female employees had academic qualifications at least equal to the *baccalauréat*, compared with 30 per cent of their male colleagues. However, unemployment is higher among women than men. They are also less likely to be promoted, and occupy less than a third of executive posts. One reason for this is that women are still almost completely responsible for household and family tasks, so they have less time and energy to devote to paid employment.

CHAPTER 8

Global Connections

Following the end of the Second World War, France and Germany formed an economic alliance that would eventually grow into the European Union (see page 13). Over the years, French governments have regarded the EU as a way of extending their power, and the French have maintained a strong influence over EU policies. France has resisted moves that might change this, for example, by twice vetoing the UK's application for membership in the 1960s.

In 2004, the central role of France was again challenged by the expansion of EU membership to 25 states. Some politicians and members of the public are concerned that elements of the French vision of Europe will be lost, for example, the building of a united Europe as a counterbalance to US power in the world.

THE INVOLVEMENT OF FRANCE IN WORLD AFFAIRS

As one of the top five economically developed countries in the world, France holds a strong position in the global economy. It has trade links with many countries, it influences international politics, and takes a significant role in world affairs through its membership of a number of international organizations. France is a member of the G8, a group of the eight leading industrialized countries which meets every year to discuss a range of current affairs of global significance. Past issues have included the fight against AIDS and the reduction of

▼ The offices of the German company Mercedes-Benz on the Champs Elysées in Paris reflect the close trade links that exist between France and Germany.

debt for many of the world's poorest countries. The G8 was first formed in 1975 by the French president of the time, Valérie Giscard d'Estaing, who invited leaders of the other top five industrial nations – Italy, the UK, the USA, Germany and Japan – to discuss world affairs in an informal way. Since then Russia and Canada have joined as permanent members. The president of the European Union attends G8 meetings, along with guests from other countries who may be invited by any of the member countries.

In 1945 France joined the United Nations (UN). Since then France has held one of only five permanent seats on the UN Security Council, which is charged with maintaining peace between nations. It was in this forum that, in 2003, France opposed the US-led declaration of war on Iraq, arguing that it went against the UN charter. France wanted to continue using a diplomatic rather than a military approach to disarm Iraq. In other circumstances, France has supported military intervention through the UN. In 2001, for example, France was in favour of sending troops to Afghanistan.

▲ Official visits, such as this of President Chirac to Tunisia in 1995, help to publicize France's global links.

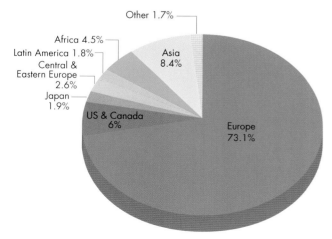

▲ Origin of imports by major trading region

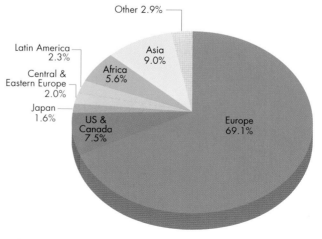

▲ Destination of exports by major trading region

France is also a member of the North Atlantic Treaty Organization (NATO). Through this military alliance, French armed forces took part in military intervention in Kosovo in 1999. In 2003 there were 34,000 French armed forces stationed in various countries of the world, including former colonies in Africa such as the Central African Republic. Most of the duties of the armed forces were in a peacekeeping capacity for the UN.

Alongside the element of international co-operation, France has always maintained an independent foreign policy. This is illustrated by the French approach to the Israeli-Palestinian conflict. France has long insisted that there can be no solution to the conflict without the involvement of the Palestinian leader (Mahmoud Abbas, who succeeded Yasser Arafat following his death in 2004).

DEVELOPMENT AID

France is one of the largest donors of development aid in the world. This is measured as a percentage of its Gross Domestic Product, and was 0.37 per cent in 2001. France gives most of its development aid to former colonies. In 2002, for example, the top five countries given aid by France were African former colonies, with Côte d'Ivoire receiving the most aid (13 per cent of the total). French companies may also benefit from the money given as aid because

 Did you know?

France still maintains strong links with countries that used to be French colonies. For many of them, France is often one of their most important trading partners. For example, Côte d'Ivoire exports coffee and cocoa to France while importing French manufactured goods.

◀ French troops assist an injured comrade in Kosovo in 1999. As a member of NATO, France was part of the military presence in the Balkans during the 1990s conflict.

▲ The world's largest passenger plane, the Airbus A380 (a prototype of which can be seen in the background) has been built in Toulouse, France. It is the result of a collaboration between France, Germany, Spain and the UK. The Airbus A380 is twin-decked and can carry up to 550 passengers.

they are often employed to carry out work on development projects. For example, a French engineering consortium won a contract worth 88 million Euros to electrify train lines in Algeria. France also contributes to UN humanitarian relief operations. In 2004, French military planes were used to transport food supplies to refugees fleeing to Chad from Darfur, Sudan.

 Did you know?

About 165 million people in the world use the French language. French is the official language in more than 30 African countries, many of which, such as Côte d'Ivoire and Senegal, used to be French colonies. Belgium, Switzerland, Luxembourg and Canada, also have French as one of their official languages.

Focus on: France as a nuclear power

France has nuclear weapons as part of its national defence. In 1995 the French carried out a series of nuclear tests, setting off underground explosions on Mururoa Atoll in the South Pacific. This is part of French Polynesia, a former colonial territory of France now politically independent, but still economically dependent on France. There were numerous local and global protests against this action. The protesters felt that France could be causing considerable damage to the environment. There was also anger that the French should carry out these potentially damaging tests far away from mainland France. Within French Polynesia, riots and demonstrations took place in Tahiti, and people in Australia, New Zealand and Japan boycotted French products, such as wine. In 1996, France made a commitment to stop testing by signing the Comprehensive Test Ban Treaty. Since then, French scientists have used computer simulations to examine the effects of nuclear explosions.

CHAPTER 9

Transport and Communications

▲ Since 1969, most of the motorways, or *autoroutes*, of France have been privately run and there are now toll booths throughout the network. Motorways provide a speedy route for those willing to pay tolls.

France has one of the longest road networks in Europe, with 894,000 km (555,174 miles) of which over 9,000 km (5,592 miles) is motorway (known as 'autoroute'). The majority of *autoroutes* are privately-run toll roads. Some of them are given names, for example, the Autoroute du Soleil (Motorway of the Sun) links Paris with the warmer regions of the Mediterranean.

France recognizes the economic importance of good transport networks and has established excellent road and rail links with other countries. Some of these have demanded considerable feats of engineering. The 50-km (32-mile) long Channel Tunnel runs under the English Channel and links France with the UK. A tunnel cut through the Alpine mountain range of Mont Blanc links France with Italy.

Car ownership is high in France. Over 80 per cent of households have one car and over 30 per cent have two or more. Diesel cars account for around a third of new car sales, a higher

Did you know?

Over 76 per cent of France's total freight is carried by road. The amount has increased by around 100 per cent since the mid 1980s, compared with a fall in freight carried by rail of about 25 per cent over the same period.

proportion than elsewhere in Europe. Diesel vehicles have been popular because they are fuel efficient, but their popularity has declined recently because they produce higher levels of pollutants than non-diesel vehicles. Air pollution is now a major concern, particularly in urban areas with high levels of traffic.

RAILWAYS

France's rail network extends for 32,175 km (19,993 miles) and includes about 4,500 km (2,796 miles) of specialized track for France's high-speed train service, the Train à Grande Vitesse (TGV). The TGV links France's largest population centres and carries 71 million of the 295 million passengers who travel by rail in France every year. Designed and built by the French, the TGV was the first high-speed train in Europe and it has significantly cut journey times on major routes. For example, in the 1970s it used to take six hours to travel between Grenoble and Paris, but today it takes just three hours.

The TGV has increased average journey speeds from about 120 km/h (74 mph) to 170 km/h (106 mph), with top speeds of over 220 km/h (137 mph) on longer journeys. In 1990 it took (and still holds) the world rail speed record for a conventional wheeled train of 515 km/h (320 mph). Despite these impressive achievements, the TGV has been criticized for being too costly. Environmentalists are concerned that the specially designed track has had considerable impact on the landscape, and in some places fragile local ecosystems have been damaged, for example, in the hills of Provence around Marseille in southern France.

 Did you know?

In 1999, the TGV record was beaten by a Japanese experimental magnetic levitation ('maglev') train that reached speeds of 581km/h (345mph), although the French still hold the record for conventional wheeled trains.

 Did you know?

France's wealthiest region, the Île de France, is at the centre of the national road and rail networks.

▼ The successful TGV technology has been bought by many countries, including Australia, Taiwan and Spain.

▲ Charles de Gaulle airport is one of two international airports that serve Paris (the other is Orly). It has three terminal complexes handling both domestic and international flights.

AIR TRAVEL

France is a large country, so domestic air travel is important. There are many small regional airports with domestic flights operating from them, as well as main airports dealing with international flights. Passenger traffic has increased by over 250 per cent in 20 years. French airports also see traffic of around 4.9 billion tonnes (4.8 billion tons) of freight per year.

URBAN TRANSIT SYSTEMS

Traffic congestion and air pollution are serious concerns in many French cities, and particularly in Paris. Here, the *métro* (subway) was first established in 1900 to handle transportation within the city centre. Today the *métro* carries around 9 million passengers daily. However, many commuters continue to travel into Paris by car. This is a trend that Régie Autonome des Transports Parisiens (RATP), the operators of public transport in Paris, have been trying to reverse for the past 30 years. In 1977, RATP linked the *métro* with the regional express rail network of trains connecting central Paris with the suburbs. In 1998, a fully automated rail line called the Meteor was added to the *métro* network. Several cities, including Lille, Lyon and Marseille, have developed light rail networks to try to reduce traffic congestion in their urban areas.

? Did you know?

The world's highest road bridge – the viaduct de Millau – opened in December 2004. The four-lane bridge crosses 270 m (885 feet) above the Tarn Valley, at the southern edge of the Massif Central, near the town of Millau in the Lanquedoc region.

FRANCE AND THE INFORMATION SOCIETY

The Internet has been relatively slow to take off in France. The reason for this, in part, is a system called Minitel, established by France Telecom twenty years ago. Minitel gives phone subscribers a terminal to access services on-line, in a similar way to the Internet. Many people in France therefore saw no need to pay for the personal computers needed for the Internet when they already had free equipment to do many of the same things. Minitel terminals are simpler than a computer, consisting of a small screen and keyboard that is connected to a phone.

However, the past ten years have seen a communications revolution, with significant growth in the use of the Internet and mobile phones. The number of people using the Internet

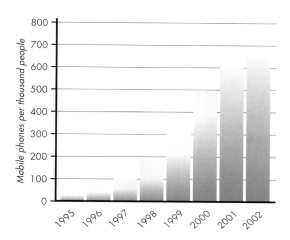

▲ Mobile phone use per 1,000 people, 1995-2002

Transport & communications data

- 📂 Total roads: 894,000 km/555,174 miles
- 📂 Total paved roads: 894,000 km/555,174 miles
- 📂 Total unpaved roads: 0 km/0 miles
- 📂 Total railways: 32,175 km/19,993 miles
- 📂 Major airports: 477
- 📂 Cars per 1,000 people: 477
- 📂 Mobile phones per 1,000 people: 647
- 📂 Personal computers per 1,000 people: 347
- 📂 Internet users per 1,000 people: 314

Source: World Bank and CIA World Factbook

increased from 2.2 million in 1997 to 19 million by 2004, and mobile phone subscribers increased from 0.8 million in 1994 to 39 million by 2004. Networks for both are highly developed in urban areas, but less so in rural areas. The development of information technology is a government priority. In 1997, the Government Action Programme for the Information Society was set up. Among other things, this programme has ensured that all secondary schools are now connected to the Internet.

Focus on: Space research

France's National Space Centre opened in 1961 to provide technical and research expertise to the space industry. France is also a member of the European Space Agency (ESA) and contributes 29 per cent of the ESA budget. The space industry accounts for some 13,000 jobs on French territory. France also hosts the ESA's launch site at Kouron in French Guiana. The ESA is not involved with manned spaceflights; instead it focuses on launching satellites to advance the fields of navigation, communication, the media and the monitoring of the global environment.

▲ This interactive science park near Toulouse has a life-size model of the European Space Agency's *Ariane 5* space rocket.

CHAPTER 10

Education and Health

Education between the ages of six and 16 has been free and compulsory in France and its territories since 1967. Pre-school education for children aged over three years had 100 per cent attendance in 2000, compared with 61 per cent in 1970. The value attached to education in French society is reflected in the funding it receives – 5.8 per cent of the Gross Domestic Product compared with the EU average of 4.92 per cent. About 80 per cent of French schools are state-run and secular; most of the remaining 20 per cent are private Catholic schools. There are two Muslim schools in France, one in Lille in northern France and one in Paris.

▼ In French primary schools teaching of the basic skills of reading, writing and arithmetic are given a high priority and children tend to sit in rows to be taught these.

THE STRUCTURE OF THE EDUCATION SYSTEM

Children go to primary school at age six and then, aged eleven, to a type of secondary school called a *collège*. A state-run *collège* takes all children from the local area, regardless of ability or background. At fifteen, students move on to a *lycée*, which may be vocational, technical or general, depending on the aptitude and

Did you know?

Until the 1980s, a national curriculum meant that all children were taught the same subject at the same time regardless of where they lived in France. However, the Decentralization Acts in 1982 and 1984 allowed *régions*, *départements*, *communes* and individual schools a say in the development of their curricula and timetables.

preference of the individual students. Those remaining at school until eighteen will take the *baccalauréat* ('*le bac*'), a programme of study first created by Napoléon in 1808. Students choose options within *le bac* so they will specialize in, for example, maths, science or philosophy while continuing to study a range of subjects. The number of students gaining *le bac* has risen from 69 per cent of those aged eighteen in 1970 to over 80 per cent in 2001. The *baccalauréat* qualification is the essential credential for entry into any of the French national universities. The percentage of those aged twenty going into higher education has risen sharply, from only 16.8 per cent in 1980 to 52.5 per cent in 2000.

Instead of university, a few students will go on to *grandes écoles*, highly prestigious institutions that have a rigorous entry examination called the *concours*. Students will have studied for the *concours* at a special *lycée*. Those who gain entry to the *grandes écoles* are likely, following graduation, to be recruited to France's highest ranking positions in government and top jobs in industry and commerce.

▲ At *collège*, teachers assess the progress of each student at the end of the year and decide whether they move up for the following school year.

VARIATIONS IN EDUCATIONAL ACHIEVEMENTS

Adult literacy rates are almost universal (99 per cent) in France, but there are some notable variations which appear to relate to socio-economic or cultural groups. Immigrant communities, for example, have lower literacy rates despite the fact that education is free to all. The government has established 'priority education areas' to provide extra funds to *collèges* that serve disadvantaged areas. In 2001, about 18 per cent of primary and 21 per cent of secondary pupils attended *collèges* in these areas.

Education and health

- Life expectancy at birth male: 75.5
- Life expectancy at birth female: 83.0
- Infant mortality rate per 1,000: 4
- Under five mortality rate per 1,000: 6
- Physicians per 1,000 people: 3.3
- Health expenditure as % of GDP: 9.6%
- Education expenditure as % of GDP: 5.8%
- Primary net enrolment: 100%
- Pupil-teacher ratio, primary: 18.7
- Adult literacy as % age 15+: 99

Source: United Nations Agencies and World Bank

HEALTH

In 2000, the World Health Organization declared that France had the best healthcare system in the world. The level of satisfaction is high, with 66 per cent of French people reporting they are happy with the care received (compared with 40 per cent in UK). There are three doctors for every 1,000 people (compared with three per 1,800 in the UK and three per 2,700 in the USA). Treatments for cancer and heart disease (two of the major killers) are impressive, with survival rates higher than in other European countries. This top-class healthcare means that life expectancy at birth for women was 83 years in 2004 (second only to Japan), and for men it was 75.5 years.

Until 2004, all French citizens could choose to see specialists without first seeing a doctor, and there were no waiting lists for hospital treatment. Costs were covered by a combination of the state's social security system and *mutuelles* (co-operative insurance bodies).

Although France spends over 9 per cent of its GDP on health there is a healthcare budget deficit of over 10 billion Euros a year, which looks set to worsen. As the ageing population puts more pressure on the system, the projected deficit by 2010 is 29 billion Euros. In spite of public opposition to changes in the health system, reforms were eventually agreed in 2004 in hopes of reducing the spending deficit by 2007. Patients now have to pay for some prescriptions, medical tests and for seeing a specialist.

▼ France has centres of excellence for medical research, such as this gene research centre at Evry, near Paris.

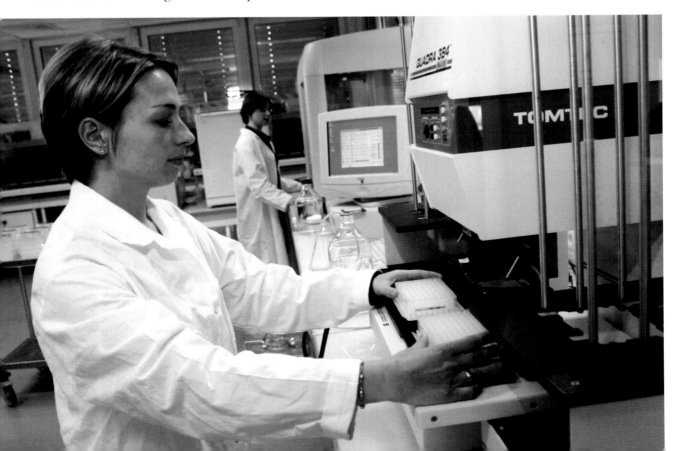

LIFESTYLE CHOICES

Some of France's most serious health problems are linked to lifestyle choices, such as drinking alcohol and smoking. French men have the highest level of cancer-related deaths in western Europe and cancer, as a cause of death, increased from 20 per cent of all deaths in 1970 to nearly 28 per cent by 1999. The death rate from heart disease decreased slightly over the same period, but is still considered to be too high. The government has increased taxes on cigarettes and launched awareness campaigns to discourage people from smoking and drinking. There has also been an increase in obesity, associated with poorer diets involving more fast food and less fresh produce.

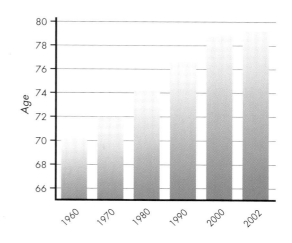

▲ Life expectancy at birth, 1960-2002

▶ Small local markets, held weekly in towns and villages, are a good source of fresh fruit and vegetables. But their importance is now challenged as more convenience and packaged food becomes available.

Focus on: The Pasteur Institute, Paris

The Pasteur Institute is one of the world's leading medical research centres, employing over 1,000 scientists. Louis Pasteur, famous for discovering the sterilization process and the vaccine for rabies, first established the institute as a non-profit research organization in 1887. Since then, eight of the institute's scientists have been awarded the Nobel Prize for medicine. The institute has been responsible for the discovery of several vaccines, including those for diphtheria, tetanus and tuberculosis. In 1983, scientists from the Pasteur Institute were the first to isolate the AIDS virus and the institute's research into HIV/AIDS continues today, benefiting not only the 0.3 per cent of adults aged between 15 and 49 affected in France, but also the millions affected in developing countries.

CHAPTER 11

Culture and Religion

▲ Traditional French cuisine uses fresh ingredients that are produced locally. In coastal areas, fish and seafood provide regional speciality dishes.

French cuisine has established a worldwide reputation for high quality and for particular delicacies such as cheeses, baguettes, crêpes and patés. The word 'gourmet' describes a person who enjoys good food and drink. The word originates from France, and most French people are indeed true gourmets. The French love of food can be seen in the use of good quality, fresh ingredients, and of local markets as popular places to shop. Until recently, sitting down to a four-course meal each day was the norm. But a government survey in 2004 indicates that this pattern is changing, with 55 per cent of those interviewed eating a smaller evening meal in front of the TV. The French habit of drinking *vin de table* (table wine) with every meal is also changing: in 1980, 430 million litres of wine were consumed, a figure that had declined to 340 million litres by 2003.

THE VISUAL ARTS

France has played an important role in the history of western art. This dates from the Renaissance in the fourteenth century, when French kings invited the finest European artists to decorate their palaces. Paris became the centre of important artistic developments, although the artists themselves were not necessarily French. In the nineteenth century, a distinctly French art movement called Impressionism had a far-reaching influence. Impressionist artists, including Edouard Manet

(1832–83) and Claude Monet (1840–1926), tried to escape the static art of the time by using a combination of light and movement in their paintings. Other schools and styles of art with their roots in France were to follow. Famous French artists included the post-Impressionist Henri Toulouse-Lautrec (1864–1901), who painted scenes from Parisian cafés, and the Cubist painter Georges Braques (1882–1963). Today France has some of the world's best art museums: the Louvre museum in Paris was visited by 6.6 million people in 2004.

France has the highest cinema audiences in Europe. The popularity of cinema in France dates back to 1895, when the world's first public picture house opened in Paris. Today, the French film industry is thriving, largely as a result of public subsidies of more than 245 million Euros a year that are given to French produced films. Many French directors, actors and actresses – for example François Truffaut, Gerard Depardieu and Brigitte Bardot – are world famous. One of the most well known international film festivals is held every year in Cannes in south-eastern France.

France has also contributed to the development of photography. In 1826, Joseph Nicéphore Niépce was the first person to produce a photographic image on paper, taking eight hours to do so. In 1839, Jacque Daguerre reduced the photographic development time to half an hour.

Did you know?

The value that is attached to cinema in French culture is reflected in the development of Futuroscope, a unique theme park about cinema, video and visual technology, that was opened near Poitiers in 1987. It now attracts about two million visitors a year.

▼ The striking glass pyramid that covers the main entrance of the Louvre museum in Paris was designed by the Chinese-born architect, Leoh Ming Pei.

ARCHITECTURE

France has a fascinating variety of architecture. There are wonderful examples of Gothic cathedrals built between the twelfth and fifteenth centuries and characterized by pointed arches, flying buttresses and stained-glass windows. Notre Dame cathedral in Paris, completed in about 1345, has spectacular rose windows and ornate flying buttresses. The chateaux of the Loire Valley are examples of lavishly decorated royal country retreats from the fifteenth and sixteenth centuries. Modern architects have also made their mark, particularly in Paris with examples such as the Pompidou Centre, built in the 1970s.

FRENCH WRITERS

There is a long tradition in France of writers tackling philosophical questions and ideas. The work of Renée Descartes (1596 –1660) marks the beginning of modern French philosophy and has influenced philosophers around the world. Other philosophers who have had a worldwide influence include Jean-Paul Sartre (1905–80), Simone de Beauvoir (1908–86) and Jacques Derrida (1930–2004). French writers have also produced novels, many of which are considered classics today: examples include *Les Misérables* by Victor Hugo (1802–85), and *L'éstranger* by Albert Camus (1913–60).

► The Pompidou Centre in Paris is designed to have its internal pipes and ducts on the outside, giving it an unusual and controversial appearance.

RELIGION IN A SECULAR STATE

In France, religion is considered to be a matter of personal choice. This separation of religion and state, called the secular principle, was established in 1905 and was further developed in 1946 when it first appeared in the constitution. The emphasis is on respecting all beliefs equally rather than being anti-religion. In recent years, racial tensions between ethnic groups with different religious beliefs have included a religious dimension and so have put the principle of secularity under pressure.

There are churches in every city, town and village, reflecting the historical importance of religion, particularly Catholicism. Around 65.5 per cent of the population say they are Catholic although fewer than one in ten go to Mass on a regular basis. Immigrant populations from North Africa (a predominately Islamic region) brought their faith with them when they settled in France. Muslims are now the second largest religious group, making up approximately 7.1 per cent of the French population. Protestants comprise around 1.2 per cent. Jews represent some 1 per cent – a higher proportion than in any other western European country.

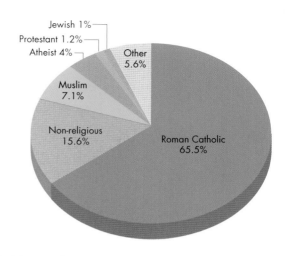

▲ Major religions

Focus on: Defending the secular principle, or racism?

In September 2004, a new law was passed banning school students, and those who work in the government's public services, from wearing obvious religious symbols, including large crucifixes, turbans and headscarves. Supporters of the law say it ensures that schools and state institutions, such as the courts, remain secular places, unaffected by religious and cultural beliefs. But opponents see it as a racist law that targets Muslim girls whose headscarves are a particularly obvious religious symbol that cannot be easily substituted with something smaller and unobtrusive. They point to the fact that Catholic students are still able to wear small crucifixes. Many Muslims feel they are being forced to choose whether they are Muslim or French. They believe the ban will encourage discrimination against Muslims.

 Did you know?

The secular nature of the school system in France means that, instead of religion, students study philosophy.

▶ There are about 1,600 mosques and Muslim prayer halls in France, but most are small makeshift premises not purpose-built places of worship like this one in Paris.

CHAPTER 12

Leisure and Tourism

The 35-hour working week introduced in 1997 (see page 32) led to a considerable increase in leisure time for many French employees. Leisure interests account for around 10 per cent of household expenditure today. The French enjoy a wide variety of leisure activities, including reading, watching TV and, increasingly, use of personal computers (PCs). In 2003, around 50 per cent of French homes had a PC, compared with 80 per cent in Sweden and 66 per cent in the UK. Increasing numbers of PCs are being sold, and French companies are now creating and marketing PC games.

▼ There are many local variations of the traditional game of *pétanque,* or *boules.* It is the fourth most popular sport in France.

Traditionally the family has been a focus of leisure time in France, with friends and family gathering to cook and enjoy meals. Although this is still true for Sunday lunches and special occasions, there has been a decline in the numbers of people spending time in this way during the week. French families also enjoy eating out. In the past there were many small family-run restaurants offering delicious food and welcoming families, but these are now under threat from the spread of fast-food chains and many small restaurants have closed.

Outside the home more people are taking an active part in sports. A survey in 2002 revealed that 66 per cent of men and 50 per cent of women participate in a sporting activity.

▲ The wide beaches along the coast near Le Havre in northern France are used for sand-yacht racing.

Popular sports include soccer, tennis, basketball and judo. The traditional game of *pétanque* (or *boules* as it is known in some regions of France) is still popular, particularly among the older generation, and most towns and villages have open-air public areas for this game to be played. A number of internationally famous sporting events take place in France every year. These include the French Open Tennis Championship and the 24-hour motor racing event at Le Mans (*24 heures du Mans*), which was first run in the 1920s. There is also the most famous bike race in the world, the Tour de France, which attracts more than 200 entrants. This race first started in 1903 and takes place over a three-week period in July. Each year the route changes, visiting different regions of France and sometimes a neighbouring country for a day or two, but it always finishes along the Champs Elysée in Paris. The Tour is extremely gruelling, covering a total distance of over 3,500 km (2,000 miles), and including steep climbs and descents in mountainous areas such as the Alps and the Massif Central.

 Did you know?

The Paris-Dakar (in Senegal) Rally, a long distance race of over 10,000 km (6,214 miles) for motorcycles, cars and trucks, has run every year since 1978. Although referred to as the Paris-Dakar Rally, the route varies occasionally with other French and, sometimes, Spanish towns hosting the start. First created by a Frenchman, Thierry Sabine, the rally now has people from over 40 nations taking part, although the majority are still French.

▲ French beaches get very crowded, particularly during the month of August when the schools have their long summer break.

THE FRENCH ON HOLIDAY

There is a French tradition of taking a long summer break in August while the schools are closed. Most French people stay in France for their holidays, and only 10 per cent go abroad. This is low compared with the Germans and British, of whom 50 and 33 per cent respectively holiday abroad, but it is higher than in the USA, where only 4 per cent of Americans holiday abroad. France offers many natural, historical and cultural attractions to tourists. Seaside holidays are particularly popular during the warm summers and have been so since the eighteenth century when they were taken to convalesce after illness. Key resorts include Biarritz on the southern Atlantic coast and Nice on the Mediterranean coast. There are also winter resorts popular for skiing and snowboarding, such as Méribel in the French Alps and Les Monts Dore in the Massif Central. Few French people take package holidays, preferring to stay instead with friends or family.

The French have the highest rate of second home ownership in Europe. Camping is popular in France, especially during the long summer vacations, as it provides cheap and convenient accommodation for families. Many towns and villages have a municipal campsite, and there are hundreds of sites in popular holiday areas such as the Mediterranean coast.

FOREIGN TOURISTS IN FRANCE

With more than 77 million foreign tourists travelling to France every year, tourism is important for the economy and is often the main source of income in rural areas such as the Massif Central. France offers foreign and domestic tourists an enormous range of attractions, including historical sites such as the Eiffel Tower (which attracts more than six million visitors a year), themed attractions such as Disneyland, Paris (with around 12 million annual visitors), and areas of great natural and scenic beauty, such as the Gorge du Tarn. Mont-Saint-Michel in Normandy combines historic and natural appeal and is one of the most visited sights outside Paris, with up to 3.5 million visitors each year.

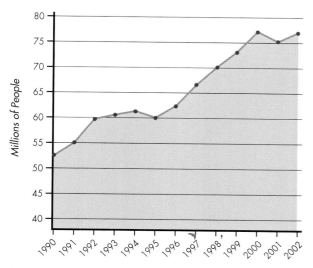

▲ Changes in international tourism, 1990-2002

Tourism in France

🗁 Tourist arrivals, millions: 77.012

🗁 Earnings from tourism in US$: 32,329,000,000

🗁 Tourism as % foreign earnings: 5

🗁 Tourist departures, millions: 17.404

🗁 Expenditure on tourism in US$: 19,460,000,000

Source: World Bank

Focus on: The Alps

Tourism in the Alps is a multi-billion dollar industry. In winter people come to ski, often staying in purpose-built resorts such as the Alps d'Huez situated in the Parc National des Écrins (a national park). In the summer many come to hike and climb. There may be up to 300 people climbing Mont Blanc in a single day. Since the late 1980s there have been concerns that this industry is threatened by global warming. Less snow has fallen, particularly on the slopes below 2,000 m (6,562 feet), and snowfalls have been occurring later in the winter, in February rather than in December. Higher temperatures in the summer months have melted ice high up in the peaks and led to increased risk of rock falls, making it dangerous for hikers. Some scientists believe that these recent changes are the result of natural variations in the world's climate rather than global warming.

▼ Tourists enjoy a barge holiday on the Canal du Midi at Olonzac, near Béziers.

CHAPTER 13

Environment and Conservation

France's natural landscape supports a variety of habitats and an impressive range of plant and animal species. There are more than 4,600 species of flowering plants, 283 types of bird and 93 species of mammals, more than in any other European country. However, many of the habitats that support these species have been damaged or destroyed by human activities, such as the expansion of farmland and the development of new transport links. As a result, several species, including wolves and brown bears, are currently endangered in France. The Pyrénées ibex and the Corsican deer are already extinct. However, France has undertaken, and continues to develop, a variety of measures to protect the environment.

PARKS AND NATURE RESERVES

There are four types of protected area covering 11.3 per cent of land in France. *Parcs nationaux* (national parks), of which there were seven in 2003, and *parcs naturels regionaux* (regional natural parks) are in areas of natural beauty that are generally sparsely populated. One example is the Parc Naturel des Cévennes, which covers 912 sq km (352 sq miles) in the Languedoc-Roussillon region. These parks aim to balance conservation of the environment with the needs of the people who live there. *Reserves naturelles* (nature reserves), numbering 144 in 2001, and *reserves biologiques* (biological reserves) are smaller in area and focus on preserving specific ecosystems. They are often located within other protected areas, for example, the Scandola nature reserve covers 1,900 hectares (just over 7 sq miles) within the Parc Naturel Regional de la Corse in Corsica.

WETLANDS

In addition to administering France's official protected areas, the Ministry of the Environment has special powers to enforce the protection of especially threatened habitats. For example, between 1960 and 1995 over half of France's wetlands had disappeared, so the ministry set up the national Action Plan for Wetlands in 1995. Wetlands cover two million hectares (7,722 sq miles) of France, and the plan provides national guidelines on how they can be better managed and conserved. The

◀ The beautiful limestone scenery of the Gorge du Tarn is one of the natural features that has led to the area being designated as a protected regional park, the Parc Natural des Cévennes.

Camargue, a fine example of wetland in southern France, is at risk from agricultural pesticides, water-borne industrial pollution and pressure from more than one million tourists who visit the area each year. The Camargue is also a regional natural park, and home to more than a thousand species of flowering plants, 50 species of fish, 15 types of reptile and many species of birds, including flamingos.

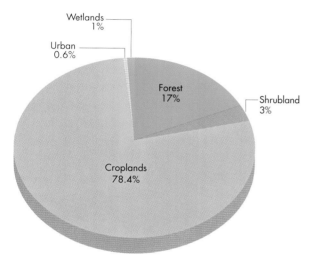

▲ Habitat type as percentage of total area

▲ A grassland fire is doused with water. Grassland and forest fires have become more frequent in some rural areas of France, such as this part of Provence.

Environmental and conservation data

▱ Forested area as % total land area: 17

▱ Protected area as % total land area: 11.3

▱ Number of protected areas: 1,153

SPECIES DIVERSITY

Category	Known species	Threatened species
Mammals	93	18
Breeding birds	283	5
Reptiles	46	3
Amphibians	39	2
Fish	169	5
Plants	4,630	2

Source: World Resources Institute

▲ Trees have been cleared from this slope to make way for a ski run. In the summer the bare slope is prone to erosion without the protection of its natural vegetation.

FORESTS

Forests and woodlands cover approximately 9.3 million hectares (35,907 sq miles) of France and are threatened by a range of activities and problems, including commercial logging and damage from acid rain. The latter is particularly a problem in the north, where there is a higher concentration of industries. Since the 1980s, the government has brought in legislation to ensure that industries pay to clean up the pollution they cause. This is known as the 'polluter pays' principle, and it has been successful in helping to reduce and control industrial air and water pollution.

MOUNTAIN REGIONS

Mountainous and alpine environments are fragile, with thin soils and steep slopes that are prone to erosion. They are easily damaged by the development of skiing facilities (ski lifts, special ski runs, hotels etc.) all of which involve felling many trees. These developments not only cause the direct destruction of habitats for wildlife and plants, some of which are only found in a very few areas, but can also lead to increased risk of landslips, avalanches and flooding. In 1991, France joined with five other Alpine countries to draw up the Convention for the Protection of the Alps to try to limit the damage. In 1997 it was agreed that under this convention no new ski resorts would be built in the Alps although there were no restrictions imposed on the expansion of existing ski resorts.

ENVIRONMENTAL DILEMMAS

Poor air quality in urban areas is a growing problem, and emissions from transport are the major source of air pollution in France. In Paris, about three million cars enter the capital daily, many of which are diesel vehicles that emit high levels of pollutants. On some days, a photochemical smog is produced when exhaust emissions react with sunlight. This smog causes a rise in health problems, such as asthma and bronchial infections. Attempts to tackle this include the government promotion of the annual 'European Car-Free Day' and the introduction of a low sulphur diesel, which reduces sulphur dioxide emissions by 90 per cent.

Emissions of greenhouse gases, such as carbon dioxide (CO_2), have been significantly reduced largely because nuclear energy has been used for 81 per cent of electricity generation. However, some environmentalists are concerned about the long-term effects of nuclear energy production. The waste produced, although extremely small in quantity, is hazardous for many years, and has to be disposed of very carefully.

▲ The spraying of pesticides and herbicides on to agricultural land leads to many environmental problems, for example the pollution of rivers when the chemicals are washed into them by rain.

Did you know?

In France, sulphur dioxide (SO_2) emissions fell by 72 per cent between 1980 and 2000, and carbon dioxide (CO_2) emissions fell by 20 per cent in the same period.

Focus on: The return of wolves to the French Alps

European wolves were once extinct in France but can now be found again, roaming areas of the Alps. In the early 1990s, a wolf pack wandered from Italy into the French Alps and, by 2004, there were about 55 wolves in ten packs living in the area between the Italian border and the Rhône Valley. The wolves are today a protected species, but their return has not been welcomed by all. Wolves have attacked and killed increasing numbers of sheep (192 cases in 1994, rising to more than 2,000 by 2002). The government has subsidized the employment of more shepherds and guard dogs, and these have reduced the killings since 2002. However, farmers say the cost to them of protecting their livestock from the wolves is too high, even with government help. They are demanding the right to shoot wolves on sight.

CHAPTER 14

Future Challenges

The increasing social tensions and religious differences are seen by some as the most pressing problem that France faces. Young people of the urban 'sink estates', where many with immigrant backgrounds live, are increasingly angry about their poor quality of life which they believe is a result of racial discrimination. Other members of French society fear that this anger is directed against the republican values of French society. Among some of these people there has been a rise in the popularity of extreme right-wing parties with racist policies. The considerable support for the Front National demonstrated in the presidential elections of 2002 shocked many French people.

▼ Many of the high-rise urban developments, such as this one in Paris, have become very run down since they were built in the 1950s.

However, this support is likely to increase if issues of inequality between different ethnic communities in France, and the anger that these generate, are not tackled.

Like other economically developed countries, such as Japan and the UK, France faces the challenge of an ageing population. With a low birth rate and higher life expectancy, the proportion of the French population over the age of 65 is increasing. Within the next fifteen years this may cause pension problems and increase the tax burden on the economically active, younger members of society. However, French productivity is high and, if this continues to rise, problems such as these could be avoided. There may be an increased burden on the health service, which some politicians feel is already costing the country too much.

▲ Members of Greenpeace stage an anti-nuclear protest during a conference on climate change in Lyon. Their banner reads: 'Nuclear energy is not the answer to the greenhouse effect'.

HEALTH AND ENVIRONMENT

The French government has launched campaigns aimed at the prevention of health problems related to the current high consumption of tobacco and alcohol. The policies already in place to discourage smoking include larger health warnings on cigarette packets and tax increases to push up the price of cigarettes.

As one of the leading industrial nations in the world, France needs to consider carefully the environmental impact of its economic activities and its high level of energy consumption. Although French greenhouse gas emissions are considerably lower than most other economically developed nations, France achieves this through a heavy dependency on nuclear energy. Fears about the safety of the nuclear industry are increasing among the French public and are causing the government to reconsider the role of this major energy source.

THE FUTURE OF EUROPE

As one of the founding members of the EU, France has had considerable influence on its nature and direction. With the EU's continuing expansion, there are fears that new member countries may only be interested in the economic benefits of the EU free-trade area and will challenge the French vision of a politically integrated Europe. Even the use of French as the EU's core language is threatened, because about 70 per cent of the new members have English as their second language. It seems that concern about the future direction of the EU has reduced French support for it. France's rejection of the new EU constitution in May 2005 caused great debate by all EU countries about what EU membership should mean. It will be interesting to see how France, a country which historically has strong political and cultural influences in the world, deals with these issues.

Timeline

15,000 BC Cave paintings found in south-west France provide evidence of early human settlers.

1500 BC The Gauls, Celtic people from central Europe, invade France.

52 BC Defeat of the Gauls by the Romans.

AD 400-500 The Romans are defeated by the Franks.

AD 771-814 The rule of Charlemagne, during which the French Empire expands into parts of Spain, Italy and Germany.

1066 William of Normandy invades England and takes control of areas of France under English rule.

1337-1453 The Hundred Years' War between France and England.

1789 The French Revolution begins with the storming of the Bastille in Paris.

1799 Napoléon Bonaparte comes to power.

1914-18 During the First World War, France is invaded by German troops; much of the fighting takes place on French territory.

1940 During the Second World War, France is occupied by Germany until liberated by Allied forces in 1944.

1951 France and Germany form the European Coal and Steel Community (which later becomes the European Economic Community).

1975 French president Valérie Giscard d'Estaing forms a group of the six leading industrial nations called the G6 (now the G8) to discuss world issues.

1990 The French high-speed train sets the world speed record for conventional wheeled trains.

1993 The European Economic Community becomes the European Union.

1995 The French government carries out nuclear testing in the Pacific. Demonstrations take place in many countries against this action.

1996 France signs the Comprehensive Test Ban Treaty and replaces nuclear testing in the Pacific with computer simulations.

1998 France wins the football World Cup.

2002 France drops its currency – the franc – in favour of the Euro, the common currency of the European Union.

2003 France opposes the invasion of Iraq, arguing for diplomatic rather than military means to deal with the situation.

2004 The highest bridge in the world is constructed in the south of France.

2005 In a national referendum French voters reject the proposed European Union constitution. Airbus the European aerospace industry, of which France is a key member and based in France, launches the A380, the world's largest passenger jet.

Glossary

Absolute rule A form of government in which the ruler has complete power.

Allies The countries, including France, the UK, Canada and the USA, that fought against Germany, Italy and Japan in the Second World War.

Arrondisement In local government, a sub-division of a *département*. There are 342 *arrondisements* in France.

Assimilation The surrender of a migrant's cultural beliefs and practices to take on those of the country into which he or she is moving.

Baccalauréat An exam taken by high school students when they are 18. Passing *le bac*, as it is known, is necessary for entry to university.

Biomass An energy source derived from organic matter that can be burned to produce heat energy. Includes wood and sewage.

BTU British Thermal Unit, a standard energy measure.

Canton In local government, a grouping of *communes* within an *arrondisement*. There are 4,054 cantons in France.

Climatologist A scientist who specializes in studying the climate.

Colonist A person living in a country controlled by another more powerful country and who originally came from that more powerful country.

Commune The lowest tier of local government.

Consortium An organization of businesses joining together for a shared purpose.

Constitution The basic political principles on which a state is governed.

Coup A sudden seizure of political power by a group of people, often led by the military.

Crêpes Pancakes made from eggs and flour, served with either savoury or sweet fillings.

Delta A natural feature that occurs where a river deposits its load of sediment at its mouth.

Democracy A system of government that involves every citizen being able to vote for representatives within the government.

Département The second level of local government after the *régions*; there are 22 *départements* in France.

Dynasty A series of rulers from the same family.

Ecosystem All the living things in an area and the physical environment in which they exist.

Élite The most powerful group in a society.

Flying buttress Part of the external structure of Gothic cathedrals, designed to support the weight of the walls and ceiling and allow the interior to be free of pillars.

Free French French people who continued to fight against German rule during the occupation of France in the Second World War.

Global warming A gradual increase in world temperatures caused by greenhouse gases.

Left-wing Describes a set of political beliefs in which the central principle is that governments should control the distribution of wealth within society to avoid inequalities between its members.

National Assembly The lower house of the French parliament (the upper is the Senate) consisting of 577 elected members, called deputies, each representing an area of France.

Quadrillion A million billion.

Racist A person, or view held by a person, that other races are not as good as their own.

Republic A country governed by elected representatives of the people and headed by a president.

Right-wing Describes a set of political beliefs in which the central principle is that the best way to distribute wealth in society is to allow individuals the freedom to make money with little or no intervention from governments.

Secular Non-religious.

Service industries Industries or businesses that provide services or sell goods to people or other industries. Also called tertiary industries, these include shops, insurance companies, transport and tourism.

Subsidies Money given by a government to support an industry when it has difficulty in making enough through its own efforts.

United Nations (UN) An international organization established after the Second World War in 1945 to work towards the maintaining of international peace and security and international economic and social co-operation.

Vetoing The act of blocking a decision being voted on in a meeting.

Further Information

BOOKS TO READ

Horrible Histories Special: France
Terry Deary and Martin Brown
(Scholastic Hippo, 2004)

Countries of the World: France
Robert Prosser
(Evans Brothers, 2005)

Letters From Around the World: France
Teresa Fuller
(Cherrytree, 2003)

Changing Face of... France
Ruth Thomson
(Hodder Wayland, 2005)

France Since 1945
Robert Gildea
(Oxford Paperbacks, 2002)

Take Your Camera: France
Ted Park
(Raintree, 2004)

Focus on Europe: France
Anita Ganeri
(Franklin Watts, 2004)

Continents of the World: Europe
David Flint
(Hodder Wayland, 2005)

USEFUL WEBSITES

www.info-france-usa.org
The site of the French Embassy in the USA. It provides a children's section and concise notes and information on many aspects of France.

www.insee.fr
The site of the French government agency, the National Institute for Statistics and Economic Studies. Some pages are in English and have useful facts and figures, including census data.

www.unicef.org/infobycountry/france_statistics.html
The UNICEF site gives a country profile of population statistics, including a focus on children.

www.earthtrends.org/
A range of statistics available for selected countries, including France.

www.economist.com/countries/France
A country briefing and articles from the journal *The Economist.*

www.tourduvalat.org
A research centre for the conservation of Mediterranean wetlands. Based at Tour du Valat in the Camargue in southern France, it provides detailed information about the Camargue as well as other areas of Mediterranean wetlands.

www.state.gov/p/eur/
The European section of the US government site.

www.odci.gov/cia/publications/factbook/
Offers the CIA facts and figures on France.

www.eia.doe.gov/emeu/cabs/france.html
www.eia.doe.gov/emeu/cabs/franenv.html
Two detailed country profiles of France provided by the US Department of Energy.

Index

Page numbers in **bold** indicate pictures.

About the Author

Celia Tidmarsh is a geography PGCE tutor at the Graduate School of Education, University of Bristol. She has taught geography in secondary schools in the UK for 15 years.

She has written a number of geography textbooks on various topics for young people, and has also carried out research into children's attitudes to nature and environmental issues.